Getting a Job as a Rural Carrier with the United States Post Office

How to do it and what to expect

By

I0483550

Ken Alden

Getting A Job as a Rural Carrier With the United States Post Office. How to do it and What to Expect

Thank you....

Thank you for downloading my book! Please review this book on Amazon.com. With your feedback, I can make the next book even better.

Table of Contents

Introduction

In the annals of history few things are more constant than the mail. Throughout the millennia of human existence the delivery of messages, goods and cargo have been one of the most important aspects of the development of civilization as we know it. It is part and parcel (if you'll forgive the pun) of global culture. It is and always has been an important piece of the communication puzzle.

You might think in this day and age that people just don't send things "snail mail" anymore and to a certain extent you would be right. Personal letters are on the decline but people still send cards on special occasions. The real money is in junk mail. Every year 200 billion pieces of mail are delivered to almost two hundred million delivery points. That's enough for every man, woman and child to get two pieces of mail every single day of the year.

And with the advent of the internet, ordering items online through websites like Amazon and eBay has proven a boon for the U.S.P.S. Around the holidays the Post Office delivers around 400 million packages. Everyday Rural Carriers leave their respective Post Offices with vehicles stuffed to capacity. Sometimes two trips are in order to get them all delivered on time.

How does the United States Postal Service handle all this traffic? Mail carriers. Both City and Rural carriers are tasked with the duty of delivering this unimaginable mountain of mail. This book will focus on getting a job for the U.S.P.S. as an RCA.

Rural Carrier Associate

What is an RCA? RCA stands for: "Rural Carrier Associate." Basically an RCA is someone who delivers the mail outside the town or city where they are located. A more in depth definition can be found at usps.com:

The Rural Carrier Associate is a non-career long-term relief position. RCA'scover for full-time career Rural Carriers when the full-timer is out due to sickleave, vacation leave, days off, etc.

The Post Office directly employs almost 700,000 people. Indirectly the Post Office is responsible for more than 8 million jobs in the United States. Those are serious numbers. Want some more numbers? In 2014 the U.S.P.S. generated almost $68 billion in revenue. That same year saw 155 billion pieces of mail processed. They have a fleet of over 200,000 vehicles, one of the largest in the world and that's not counting the personal vehicles of the RCAs. The Post Office has around 32,000 locations nationwide. And the last number? Zero. That's how many tax dollars the Post Office received last year. That's right, the Post Office is self-sufficient. It's a multibillion dollar industry that is always on the lookout for good people. People like you!

So what do all those six and seven figure numbers mean for you personally? It means you have a darn good chance of getting a job with the United States Postal Service. Each year about 40,000 new postal employees are hired to replace those who retire, die (that is the sad truth), and are a part of just general turnover. That's 40,000 new jobs every year! Or 110 new jobs every day. While not all those jobs are RCA positions, a good portion of them are. Very few industries have these kinds of opportunities for job seekers.

So, who am I and what qualifies me to tell you how to get an RCA position? I happen to be currently employed as an RCA with the U.S.P.S. I have been a carrier for almost six years and know the good the bad and the ugly of the job. I know the process. I've taken the tests and done the work. I know what it takes. I've written this book to help you decide if the job is right for you. And I will be honest here - It is not an easy job and it isn't right for everyone. That being said if you move forward with your decision to get a job as an RCA, I will guide you through the process and tell you exactly what to expect every step of the way - *before and after* you are hired.

This book includes the following information:

- An unbiased look at what the job is and is not.
- What to expect.
- How to find listings for positions.
- How to apply.
- How to Take and pass the 473E test.
- The interview.

- Background checks and driving records.
- Orientation.
- Rural Academy.
- Getting the right vehicle as well as a discussion on the postal vans known as "LLVs" (Long Life Vehicles).
- Your duties as an RCA.
- Doing your job throughout the year.
- Your probationary period.
- How to move forward in your career
- And a host of other topics that will give you a leg up on other applicants and ease the pain of the hiring process.

Working for the Post Office is a great opportunity. And the fact that you have purchased this book tells me you are thinking the same thing. The Postal Service is always hiring new RCA's. Don't let that statement scare you. When an entity employs hundreds of thousands of people turnover is a fact of life. Don't see it as a red flag view it as an opportunity to move forward.

Getting a job, any job with the Postal Service is a long, drawn out and complicated process. But for those willing to make the effort and invest the time the payoff is well worth it. You must be patient. The government never does anything with haste.

But it's like the old saying goes - Good things come to those who wait. I think most of us would agree a good job is worth waiting for.

There are a lot of resources available for those seeking a position with the Postal Service. Most glorify the job so they can sell you a product that "guarantees" you will get the job. There are no guarantees. The only thing I will guarantee, as a current RCA, is that the information provided in this book will help you decide if the job is right for you - no sugar coating - and what to expect along the journey. I can provide a perspective others cannot.

So, if I haven't scared you off yet, let's get started! The mail waits for no one!

Chapter One

What does an RCA do?

In the introduction I briefly defined what a rural carrier is and does. In this chapter, I want to expand that definition and talk more about the day to day duties of this position. Like I've mentioned already this is not an easy job. But if you give yourself time to learn it you will likely enjoy it.

Disclaimer: I am not going to teach you how to do the job. That is not the purpose of this book. I want to explain the basics so you know what to expect as you make your journey from applicant to employee.

Your job as an RCA is to deliver the mail. How do you get that done? There is a multi-step process. When you arrive in the morning you will go to your case. RCAs don't use a time clock. They either write their time down on what is called a "green card" or they fill in their name and time on a white time sheet that is kept in the case where you and the regular will be working. Once this is done you will start casing your mail.

Casing your mail means you are sorting the mail you will deliver into a case where each slot is marked with the address you will deliver to, in the order you will deliver it. Below is a picture of a typical case:

Figure 1 A Mail Case

As you can see there are slots for the mail. This will be the most time consuming and frustrating thing to learn on your new job. It is one of the biggest reasons new hires wash out. You will be sorting "raw mail." Raw mail is mail that for some reason or another was kicked out of the sorting process and must be sorted by hand into the case. If you aren't familiar with the case and where everything is located, this can be a real headache. You will also be working with presorted mail called "DPS".

DPS stands for **"Delivery Point Sequence."** Basically, what this means is that most of your mail comes in trays pre-sorted in the order of delivery. You have the option of not casing this mail and taking it to the street. I would advise against that until you get comfortable with the whole process of sorting, casing and delivering.

After you case your mail you will than sort through your parcels. Small parcels that may fit in a mailbox usually go in a tray or tub depending on your preference. We call these **"spurs."**

Bigger parcels that need to be carried to the door will go in the back of your vehicle. These are called, well, parcels. You will put a marker in the slot with the mail where the parcel is to be delivered (you would do the same thing with your spurs). This is to remind you when you get to a certain address on your route that this person has a package delivery. Make sure to mark all parcels correctly and pay attention on the route when they come up. If you miss one you will have to take the time to turn around and deliver it.

Once this is done you will check your **holds**. These are people, for whatever reason, who have requested that their mail not be delivered for a certain amount of time. You will pull these down and put them in a tray or tub under your case.

Then you will check for mail that needs to be forwarded and mail that needs to be pulled and dealt with in some other fashion. *I am purposefully being vague at this point as this is all a process that will be taught to you after you are hired. Right now I am just trying to give you an overall view of the job.*

Once you have done all this you will "**pull down**" or "**tear Down**" your mail. What this means is you will pull the mail from the slots starting with the beginning of your route and ending at the final delivery point. You will usually pull down until you have a comfortable handful and put a rubber band around it and set it into a tray. Once you are finished you will load your trays in your vehicle along with your parcels and head out to your designated route.

Once you reach the beginning of your route you start **delivering the mail**! This is the most enjoyable part of the job, in my opinion. No one is looking over my shoulder and I get to be out of the office and out on the open road. Some carriers listen to music or just enjoy the silence. I listen to audio books to help pass the time.

There's no rocket science with this part of the job. Just put the mail in the box and take the parcels to the door. Keep doing this until everything is delivered. Always pay attention to where things are going so no wrong deliveries are made.

Once all the mail is delivered, head back to the office, stack the empty trays and tubs and sort the outgoing mail and parcels. Put away your scanner and anything else you brought back with you from the route. On a typical day this is when you would sign out on your sheet and head home. Your day is done!

That is a basic description of what an RCA is and does.

What can you expect overall? As with most jobs there are positives and negatives. Here is a quick list of the pros and cons of the job:

Pros:

- **Good Pay** - Depending on your location, pay can range anywhere from $16-20 an hour.
- **Steady Work** - We will always need mail carriers so the work is always there.
- **No College Degree Needed** - You don't need a bachelors degree just common sense and a willingness to learn and work hard.
- **The Ability to Work Outside Part of the Time** - I love being outside. This is a plus for this job but, as you will see, it can also be a minus.
- **Largely Unsupervised** - Once you leave the office you don't have anyone looking over your shoulder.
- **No Set Hours** - The quicker the job is done the sooner you can go home.
- **Opportunities for Advancement and Transfer to Anywhere in the US** - Advancement can come fast if you are willing to move. Otherwise you might be an RCA for a while. *More about this later.*
- Those are some of the good things that come with the job. Now for the Cons.

Cons:

- **Being Outside** - Weather can make your day awesome or it can literally be a nightmare. The Post Office does not cancel delivery because it snowed or its 20 degrees below zero. Remember the unofficial motto is *"Neither snow nor rain nor heat nor gloom of night stays these couriers from the swift completion of their appointed rounds."* So be prepared to be hot, cold, wet and occasionally miserable.
- **Using your Own Personal Vehicle to Deliver the Mail** - As an RCA you will be expected to use your own personal vehicle to do your job. Yes, you may occasionally use a Post Office owned vehicle (aka LLV) but mostly you will be sitting in your own car. We will discuss this more fully in a later chapter.
- **The Hours** - Sometimes the hours are long and the days stretch endlessly. It's part of the job.
- **Time Constraints** - You are expected to be back by a certain time. Each route is evaluated to only take a certain amount of time to sort and deliver. You are paid according to those hours. For example: If

the route is evaluated at eight hours and it takes you six hours you still get paid for eight hours. If it takes you nine hours than you still only get paid for eight hours. The only exception to this is when you are a new hire or its around the holidays.

- **Being Considered a "Non Career Employee"** - When you are hired as an RCA you are considered a "Non Career Employee." This means until you become a "regular" you will not qualify for most benefits. You are an independent contractor of sorts. Advancement is based on seniority, meaning it might take five to ten years to become a regular with your own assigned route.

- **No Guaranteed Hours** - As an RCA you are not guaranteed hours overall. You are only guaranteed the Saturdays your primary is off. Your primary is the carrier and route you are assigned to as the main substitute carrier. This does not mean you will hardly ever work. You can cover for other regulars, learn many different rural routes, and work out of other nearby Post Offices.

- **Being "On Call"** - Calls for work can come at any time. I can't tell you how many times I have received a phone call at 6:00 AM informing me I am scheduled to report for work in a little over an hour. Typically, warnings come the night before a few days before - but not always. This is life as an RCA. Whatever you do don't say no very often, or the Postmaster may start looking for your replacement. Remember, when you get these calls they are not asking, they are telling. The only time you are not required to go in is if someone from an office that is not your home office requests your help.

Both of these lists are short and I'm sure many carriers could add or subtract from both. Lots of this stuff is my personal perspective. Individually we decide what is a pro and con for ourselves.

So those are the basics. The ups and downs and the pros and cons. The good the bad and the ugly...you get the point. The next few chapters will discuss the basic aspects of getting hired and doing the job. So, if you still think the job is for you let's move on!

Chapter Two

Finding a Job and the Application Process

So where do you start? Finding job listings for the Postal Service is easy. If you get online and type in a query about job openings with the Post Office you will get more results than you know what to do with. Your best bet, however, is to go to the source itself - the U.S.P.S. Their website allows you to peruse their listings by zip code allowing you to find where they are hiring in relation to where you live or want to live. Here is the link: "https://about.usps.com/careers/welcome.ht m"

On their website you will find not only job listings but information on the different positions, pay and benefits. I suggest reading it all. Being too well informed is not something you need to be concerned with. Knowledge is power.

You will need to open an account if you want to apply for any positions you may find of interest. To apply for a job at the U.S.P.S. you must do it through *their* website. The site features a Careers and Employment section which has an easy to use searchable database of all current vacancies. You can search for jobs on the website but if you want to apply for one you need to create an account on the website. To do this simply go to the website and fill in your details.

All you need is your name, email address and a user name. Once this information is provided you can add a resume and job history to your candidate profile later. It's not complicated. Just follow the prompts and the system will tell you what information you need to provide.

Searching for Vacancies

Once you have begun setting up your candidate profile you can search for job vacancies by location or position. As this book focuses on the RCA position, that's what you would be looking for (unless something else catches your eye). For example, you could look for jobs in California, any jobs in administrative support, or jobs in administrative support in California. It's pretty simple. You can also use keywords to search for something specific.

Applying

Once you have created your account as well as a career profile and found the position you want to apply for, all you need to do is fill in the application form and submit it. When you are filling out the application be sure to double check that you have adequately indicated how your skills, education and experience meet the specific conditions for the position you are applying for. Also, check for spelling and grammar. You never get a second chance to make a first impression.

Make sure to upload a resume with your application. If you don't have one I highly recommend you make one. If you are a veteran then you already have an advantage. The Postal Service gives priority to hiring those who have served in the Armed Forces.

I've mentioned before that this process takes time. Once you have submitted your application, resume and any other necessary information and documentation it can take anywhere from 2-6 weeks to hear back. Be patient.

Your Qualifications: A review

So just for review here are the basic qualifications you need to meet to get hired:

- Must be at least 18 years old
- Must be either a U.S. Citizen or have Permanent Alien Resident status in the U.S.
- Must NOT have taken Postal Exam 473 in the past 120 days
- Must have a valid driver's license as well as a clean driving record (this applies to mail carriers only)
- Must be able to pass a drug test
- Must have the ability to speak and read basic English
- Must be able to lift 70 pounds. *Not all positions require this but the RCA job does.*

If you meet all of these qualifications, congratulations, you already have a leg-up on a lot of potential applicants. The application process is a bit long and drawn out but it's not complicated. Be patient and don't give up. I know I say "be patient" a lot and this probably won't be the last time you read that phrase in this book. But it can take weeks and even months to get through it all and get hired.

Keeping that in mind from the beginning will make it a little easier. After all, that's the point of this book, making sure you know what to expect.

Once you have submitted your application and resume you can go back to the U.S.P.S. website and check on the status of your application. Also, keep an eye on your email as that is how they will communicate when it's time to take the next step in the application

Watch out for scams! When you get online you will find a ton of websites willing to sell you products and services that will "guarantee" to get you a job with the Postal Service. Some of them ask hundreds of dollars for information that is either free or very cheap. Some just take your money and run. There's nothing wrong with buying practice tests from reputable sources, or even a book or two to get you oriented. But stay away from expensive programs that make outrageous claims. Save your money. Keep it free and cheap and you will get all the information you need.

process. Don't neglect this. Once they send an email requesting a call to make an appointment you only have so much time to respond. If you don't do so in the allotted time they will move on to the next person on the list. **Be vigilant!**

The Test

To become a Rural Carrier Associate for the United States Postal Service you will be required to take and pass a test. Yes, I said a test. The test is called the 473E. This is a proctored exam taken on a computer at a predetermined date and location**. This is a test you must prepare for!** Approximately 80-90% of participants fail the first time they take the test. You must study!

What's on the test? Below is a basic breakdown of what you can expect:

- **Part A: Address Checking** - You will be allowed 11 minutes for this section of the test. There are 60 questions. You will be shown two sets of an address and a zip code and must decide if the two addresses are identical or different. The two lists are a "Correct List" and a "List to be Checked". The answers are as follows:

a. No Errors (both zip and address)
b. Address Only (zip codes are identical, but there is an address error)
c. Zip Code Only (addresses are identical, but there is an error in the zip code)
d. Both (both have errors)

Caution! You will be penalized for any incorrect answers on this section of the exam.

- **Part B: Forms Completion** – You are allowed 15 minutes for this portion, you will need to answer 30 questions and identify the correct way to complete each form. Pay attention to the wording of the forms. 15 minutes is plenty of time for this section so don't get in a hurry here.

There is no penalty in this section for answering; it's best to make a guess on this section, even if you are unsure of your answer. Don't leave anything blank.

- **Part C, Section 1: Coding** - This section only allows 6 minutes and is the shortest time allotment of all the sections. But it still contains plenty of material. 36 questions will be asked and you must use the proper code to assign to all addresses. You are allowed to look at the delivery route chart during this section of the exam.

Caution! You will be penalized for any incorrect answers on this portion of your exam. But you are NOT penalized for unanswered questions.

- **Part C, Section 2: Memory -** In this section of the exam, you have to memorize assigned codes for address ranges for 36 questions within 7 minutes. This is the most difficult section of the exam. Make sure to spend extra practice time here when you prepare.

Caution! You will be penalized for any incorrect answers on this portion of your exam. But you are NOT penalized for unanswered questions.

- **Part D: Inventory of Personal Experiences and Characteristics -** You will need to identify personal experiences and characteristics that are job-related. This is to determine whether or not you have the right personality to work for the US Postal Service.

There are no right or wrong answers in this part of the exam. However, since this part of the test is given prior to the proctored part, I assume your answers are analyzed for fitness as an employee of the USPS.

This not an easy test. Don't make the mistake of thinking you won't need to study. It tests your memory and ability to find mistakes under pressure. So, basically you have 90 minutes to answer 236 questions. That means you have an average of 38 seconds to answer each question. Part "A" breaks down to 11 seconds a question, which is a rapid fire pace. The test is only given once a year. That's a long time to wait for a second chance. So study!

In sections "A" and "C" you are penalized for wrong answers but not blank ones. So leaving a question blank is better than guessing and getting it wrong, to a point. The Post Office grades the test on the number of correct out of the number answered, not the ones not answered. But there is a minimum number that must be answered and the Post Office keeps that secret. So do as many as you can but don't worry if one or two don't get answered, you won't be docked for those.

Section "D" is the only part of the test that is not proctored and you will be able to take it at home. This is a personality and prior skills assessment. You have to answer all questions in this section. You are sent an email after applying for a position that requires that you take the 473E test. This email will contain a URL (Web Address) and information about creating a personal profile on a partner site that will administer this section of the test.

You need to finish this in the time allotted! You will not be able to make the appointment for the proctored sections of this exam until this part is complete. Your testing center will be busy and there may only be a limited amount of days available per week at that site to test. Don't put it off. Finish this section and make your appointment!

The Personality Assessment portion (section D) carries a lot of weight. You will be asked questions about how you react to being under pressure. How you react to others who may be behaving in a negative manner. Do you have a temper? Do you like to fight? Can you be nice when someone is being rude?

A question may look something like this:

Do you ever get in fights?
*Very often
*Often
*Sometimes
*Rarely
*Never

Be honest and answer all the questions. This is one part of the test you will not know how you were scored on. No right or wrong answers, they just want to know who you are.

It's very important to check your email daily. Make sure you are using a reliable email address for your profile. If a spam filter deletes these emails you are in trouble. You will not get a second.

So, how will your test be scored and how do you know you passed? Test 473E is scored on a scale from 0 to 100 points. You will receive a score somewhere in that range for your exam. A passing score is 70. However, your test score is not the same as the number of questions you answer correctly. You will receive a bonus five points if you are a military veteran. The test is tough and most people who pass score in the mid to high seventies. The high end these days is mid to high eighties. Another indication of the need to study.

There are lots of free websites to take practice exams. Cheap books can be found at online retailers like Amazon. Like I've said before, this is not a training manual. I'm just telling you about the process and what you can expect. Get a study guide. You won't be sorry you did. You cannot over prepare.

The Interview

Like any job you will go through an interview process before you are hired. And, like any job, you must perform well at this stage if you expect to gain employment with the Postal Service. You will get an email or possibly a phone call asking you to schedule an interview. Keep an eye on your email account and return any phone calls you may have missed promptly. The interview will usually be scheduled within a few days of contact.

Dress nicely and present a professional and personable demeanor. This is no fluff interview. You will be asked about your skills, experience, education and how you plan to apply your skills to a job at the Post Office.

You will be asked how you react under pressure. Can you be nice when someone's being rude. How would you react if your supervisor is rude and unreasonable? My interview lasted an hour.

They are thorough so be prepared to talk about yourself in a way you might find uncomfortable. Don't let this stress you out. If you've made it this far you have a good shot at getting the job. Just relax and tell them why you are the best candidate for the position.

They will ask you about past employers. Be honest but don't bad mouth your former bosses. They will ask if you can work odd hours. Your driving record and criminal history will be discussed. You absolutely must be honest here. They check. If they find you have lied on your application it will be withdrawn from consideration. Just because you have a speeding ticket doesn't necessarily mean you won't get the job so there is no reason to try and hide it.

Be upbeat and positive. No one wants to hire someone who will bring down the morale of the office. Let them know you have what it takes to be a great employee from the start. A positive attitude sometimes says a lot more than mere words.

The Checks

I touched on it earlier: You will have your background checked and your driving record pulled - nationally, not just the state you live in. If you have any criminal convictions they will find them. The kicker is that you will be asked beforehand so you must answer honestly. The same goes with your driving record. All 50 states will be checked. So if you got a speeding ticket while you were on vacation in Hawaii and then went back home to Texas they will find it.

No one knows for sure what will and will not get your application pulled. But there are a few things to keep in mind as they are serious red flags to those who makes the decisions. Felonies in the recent past might be something that will get you booted. A DUI on your driving record is a big reason why many people don't get hired. To reiterate: **You will be asked! Be honest!**

Once you've passed the test, aced the interview, and the background checks come back clean, you will be asked to take a drug test. I'm sure most of us have done this before so it's nothing new. You will get an email requesting you go down to your local testing facility and urinate in a jar. Simple right? Yes, but with a catch. Once you get that email you have a small window of time, three to four days to get it done. If you miss that window your application will be withdrawn. So keep an eye on your email and go in as soon as you possibly can. Don't procrastinate.

How Long Does All This Take?

There is no specific answer to this question. As you read this chapter it sounds like it all goes by pretty fast but I assure you it doesn't. From the time I applied to the time I was hired was about two months. That was considered pretty fast. I've known people who waited nearly a year after taking the test before they started the rest of the process. That might be extreme, but the Federal Government never does anything quickly. It might be weeks, months or even a year. It all depends on where you live, how many job openings there are and how many people apply.

The key is patience.

Time passes, you've jumped through all the hoops and one fine day they tell you you're now officially an employee with the United States Postal Service! Great! Congratulations! Now what?

Orientation! That three day ordeal all new hires must endure before they get to move on to the next step. In chapter three I will let you know what to expect at this stage of the game.

Chapter Three

Orientation

Now that you've been hired you will get a notification of your orientation dates and be shipped off for a three day snooze fest the Post Office calls "Orientation." Don't worry you get paid while you are there as well as the miles you commute to and from the orientation site. I'm sure most of us have been through orientations before. This one is no different in most respects but does have a few unique aspects.

It will most likely be in a classroom type setting with as many as 20 other new hires. Not all will be there for the same job. At the Post Office the different departments are called "Crafts." Letter Carriers are one Craft, Clerks are another, etc. You may have RCAs as well as City Carriers, Clerks and Plant Workers in the same orientation class.

Throughout the three days you will learn about the Post Office and its function. As well as how it operates and what's expected of you. Rules and regulations are discussed, and safety is pounded into your brain. You will be handed endless amounts of forms, paperwork and booklets to read. And on day three, those who may drive a postal vehicle, are treated to a daylong drivers ed course.

The first day starts with a swearing in ceremony. Yes that's right, you must take an oath of office very similar to the President of the United States. It reads like this:

"I, _____, do solemnly swear (or affirm) that I will support and defendthe Constitution of the United States against all enemies, foreign anddomestic; that I will bear true faith and allegiance to the same; that Itake this obligation freely, without any mental reservation or purpose ofevasion; and that I will well and faithfully discharge the duties of theoffice on which I am about to enter."

Your days will also be filled with power point presentations. Safety videos and even a welcome presentation from the Postmaster General Herself. Other topics like what to wear, what not to wear, what kinds of shoes you should have and so on will also be covered. As a side note, you will not have a uniform like city carriers do. You are allowed to wear street clothes on your rural rounds.

Expect to be finger printed and have your picture taken for your new ID badge. That's the norm for any government job these days. They need to have records on anyone and everyone they hire. Your badge will be useful in any and all duties you perform, so don't lose it.

Most of your orientation will revolve around Human Resource stuff as well as safety and conduct. If you've been through job orientations before much of this is par for the course.

Ask questions. This is important. They are going to throw a ton of information at you and it can get a little confusing. Take notes as you go. Again, with so much information it's going to be nearly impossible to remember everything.

Your orientation will most likely be taught by a carrier. Someone who is actually in the field doing the job. But this might not always be the case. You may get a Postmaster or supervisor. They will be knowledgeable and can, hopefully, answer your questions and get you pointed in the right direction.

Each day of orientation lasts about 7-8 hours. You will start around 7:30, depending on who is running the show and end sometime around three with a half hour lunch break. Again these schedules may vary from place to place and person to person but that's close enough for government work.

Orientation is informative and despicably boring. Bring some coffee and try not to doze off. Seriously. Our driving instructor was snoring through the driver safety power point. I guess it happens to the best of us.

As boring as it is, thankfully orientation is a breeze. It is a nice break from the hoop jumping of the hiring process and the maelstrom that will be your on-the-job training. Enjoy it, it's the last peace and quiet you will get at the Post Office for a while.

Chapter Four

The Rural Academy

After orientation you will most likely go to what the U.S.P.S. calls the "Rural Academy." This is where you start learning some of the skills it will take to do your job. I am going to burst a bubble right now: It's a complete waste of time. Well, maybe that's too strong a statement, but about 90% of it is a waste of time.

The Rural Academy lasts four days and will most likely be taught by a rural carrier who knows how the job is supposed to be done. It will be three days of classroom and one day of LLV training (the boxy, right hand drive vehicles most carriers use). Like orientation, you will be paid for your mileage to and from the training location as well as for the hours you spend in class.

You will get to case some mail but it is nowhere near the casing you will do once you reach your home office and start doing it for real. You will learn to mark packages and read labels on envelopes and parcels. You will also dive in to the world of acronyms. The government loves acronyms and the Post Office is no different. You will see ones like:

- NMR= No Mail Receptacle
- UNK= Unknown
- VAC= Vacant
- UBBM= Undeliverable Bulk Business Mail
- NSN= No Such Number
- UTF= Unable to Forward

The list goes on. You will learn that some of these acronyms can only be used on certain kinds of mail. You will learn to use the throwback case which is where many of these pieces of mail will end up. The throwback case is a case with a number of slots where endorsed mail (the ones with acronyms) and missorted mail go - both in and out of your home zip code.

You will learn how to use a handheld scanner. This piece of equipment is what is used to keep track of deliveries of parcels and certified letters. You will also scan express deliveries and other assortment of labels and forms. It is handy and can save you time but like a lot of technology it can also be a pain in the neck.

Figure 2 A U.S.P.S. Scanner

A good part of the four days at Rural Academy will be spent doing these things. Most of what you learn will likely be forgotten the moment you step out the door. If you have an understanding Postmaster (like I did) they will know this and take it into account, so don't worry about it. Just do the best you can with the time you are given.

Somewhere around the time you start the Rural Academy you are supposed to get a Shadow Day. A Shadow Day is where you will drive around with the regular carrier you are assigned to substitute for and learn the route and the job. You will learn much more doing this than you will at the Academy. Sometimes this happens before you go to Academy and sometimes after. And, unfortunately, sometimes not at all.

I shadowed another substitute on another route, which, don't get me wrong, was very helpful, but it didn't help on the route I was assigned to. This was supposed to last three days. If it happens the way it's supposed to, it will go like this:

- The first day you ride with your assigned carrier all day.
- The second day you will do the first half of the route.
- The third day you will do the second half of the route.
- After that you will be expected to carry the whole route.

Most newbie's need to be rescued the first few times since delivery must occur by a certain time and speed only comes with practice. That's okay while you're training, but they do expect you to be able to case and carry the route without help at some point in the near future. We will talk about your first week doing the actual job and what to expect in a later chapter.

At some point during your time at Rural Academy you will need to bring in the vehicle you plan to use to deliver mail for inspection and training. They basically look inside to make sure it will work for delivering mail (this applies to both left and right hand drive vehicles.) They will check the various light systems to make sure they work. Then have you drive your vehicle around to ensure you can pull up to a mailbox without hitting it. This all takes about 15 minutes. Pretty painless - unlike the LLV training.

On your fourth day (unless you schedule it for another day) you will spend the day training in an LLV. An LLV is the right hand drive vans that look a little like ice cream trucks but instead of Eskimo Pies they bring you bills and Fingerhut catalogs. This training lasts about seven hours and consists of a number of things.

First you will need to make sure you bring your driver's license. This is imperative as you will not get to train without it, they will send you home and they will not be happy about it.

Your day starts going over the LLV. You will inspect it. Tires, lights, brakes, horn etc. You will look for damage and anything else that might keep it from being ready for the work day. You will check the mirrors. The LLV has six of them and you will be expected to know how to adjust them and use them. They do take some getting used to so take your time.

After you inspect the LLV and adjust the mirrors you will get to drive it around a practice track - usually set up in some back parking lot no one uses. They have faux intersections with stop signs and places to practice backing up. Mail boxes are set up and you practice pulling up to them and putting mail in. This part lasts about three hours.

The next part is real world driving. You will spend a couple of hours driving through whatever town or city you are training in. Your instructor will give you directions as you drive. Treat it like a driving test from your local DMV because that's what it amounts to. Do exactly as your instructor says and never argue with them about driving technique. Watch your speed, use your mirrors and come to a full and complete stop at all stop signs and signals and you should be fine.

After you get back from your LLV training you are done with Rural Academy. You are ready to go home and get to work. Remember you may start at your local Post Office before you do your LLV training so don't think you will not get to work until you train on an LLV. You just won't get to drive one until it's been done.

During your time in the Rural Academy you will be approached by a Union representative. Rural carriers are represented by The National Rural Letter Carriers Association. You are not obligated to join. Nor will I tell you you should or should not be a member. This is a personal choice you must make for yourself.

Well, vacation time is over and the real work begins. In chapter six, I will discuss what to expect your first week and beyond. But first let's talk about vehicles.

Chapter Five

Postal Vehicles

Vehicles are the backbone of the United States Postal Service. With a fleet of over 200,000 vehicles the Post Office boasts one of the largest fleets in the world. This number does not count the thousands of personally owned vehicles or POV's that are used every day by rural carriers across America. In this chapter we will discuss the kinds of vehicles you may drive - both owned by the U.S.P.S. and yourself. We will talk about what to expect, what to look for when purchasing a vehicle, and all the other things that go into the transportation portion of your job.

Lets start with the vehicle you will most likely operate if you drive one owned by the Postal Service: an LLV. The LLV is one of the small vans you see driving around that look a little like an ice cream truck. LLV stands for Long Life Vehicle. The name comes from the fact that the vehicle was supposedly designed to last at least twenty years.

The LLV was made by Grumman, an aircraft manufacturer in Long Island New York. The chassis was made by General Motors and sports an inline four-cylinder that gets it down the road on suspension based on Chevy's Blazer. They are two-wheel drive vehicles, and can be a real pain in the neck on snowy days. There are some good things and some bad things you need to know about the LLV.

The bad:

- They are loud.
- There is no insulation and they rattle like a tin can with marbles. This is especially true on rough roads.
- You will bake in the summer as there is no air conditioning (just a dash fan)
- You will freeze in the winter. There is a heater but with the giant window open all day it does little good.
- The seat is uncomfortable and half the time you feel like you are going to slide out the window.
- Depending on the age and condition of the vehicle they can be gutless and slow. But after 100,000 plus miles of being beaten day in and day out I guess I would feel gutless and slow too.

The good:

- Very tight turning radius makes them a breeze to turn around.
- Large side window makes it easy to service any mailbox.
- A huge side door makes for easy entry and exit. I'm over 6' tall and have no problem with this door.

- A large cargo area makes it a snap to organize your mail and parcels for delivery. Remember this van was designed specifically for the United States Postal Service and does that job well.
- It isn't built for comfort, it's built to get the mail out in an efficient and quick manner. All in all, with a few draw backs, it does the job admirably.
- The best thing about an LLV? It's not yours! When you drive an LLV you aren't putting miles on your vehicle and adding to the wear and tear, which in this business can be substantial.

How often will you be required to drive an LLV? This is a question that can only be answered in the most basic terms. Depending on your office you may drive them a lot or never drive one at all. Offices differ in how many LLVs they have. I have heard of offices where everyone drives one and I have heard of others where the office doesn't have a single LLV. So it will vary.

LLVs are assigned to routes not carriers. So if you get put on a particular route that has an LLV assigned to it you will be parking your personal vehicle for the day. In my office I drive one a lot. In another office, it may be the same or not at all. Some people hate them. Some people love them. I only like them. They do what they are supposed to do with no bells or whistles. That, friends, is the LLV in a nutshell.

Personally Owned Vehicles

A vehicle you own and maintain will be what you drive most of the time as you do your job as a rural carrier. The Postal Service will reimburse you at the rate of $.69 a mile or a minimum of $27.80 a day whichever is greater. This does not cover all the costs associated with your vehicle - but it helps.

You will need a vehicle that is dependable and can do the job. A vehicle you own right now may be used to carry the mail, but it will have to have certain qualifications. Most of us own a left hand drive vehicle. Many carriers have driven them for years. Maybe you've seen them sitting in the passenger seat and steering with their extended left arm? It can be done in the right vehicles.

If this is what you plan on doing you need to know a couple of things. First, a vehicle with bucket seats and middle console will nearly always make driving a left hand drive from the passenger seat impossible. The reason is that you cannot safely operate the pedals with a middle console. There are kits that allow you to install pedals on the right hand side which would help eliminate this issue. There are also kits that will allow you to put a steering wheel on the right hand side of the car. These kits are a little pricy and can run up words of $1,800 for a full kit. Another thing to keep in mind is it must be an automatic transmission. It's impossible to drive a manual transmission from the right hand side and no kit I've ever seen moves the clutch pedal.

If you decide to use your left hand drive vehicle be prepared to have your vehicle inspected during Rural Academy. You will also be asked to drive it from the right hand side to see how you perform. They will tell you then and there if you will be able to use your car on the job.

If you plan to purchase a right hand drive, and I highly recommend you do as it will simplify your life immensely, there are a few things you need to know.

Right hand drive vehicles are not hard to find if you look. The first place to start looking is the Post Office where you will be working. There are always carriers who are retiring or have been assigned a route where they will be using an LLV and don't need their right hand drive vehicle anymore. It seems someone always knows someone who is selling a right hand drive rig. If you strike-out at your local Post Office, get on Craigslist. You can scour the entire country if necessary to find one. Your local papers, eBay and other online sources may also be an option. There are websites dedicated to selling postal vehicles to rural carriers. They are out there and usually within nearly anyone's budget.

So what are you going to find once you start looking? There are a number of options available. First you will notice that most of the right hand drive vehicles you come across will be Jeeps. Most of them are either Wranglers or Cherokees. These are not ex-postal vehicles but straight from the manufacturer to the public rigs. You used to be able to find the old postal jeeps pretty easy but they are becoming harder and harder to find and the prices on them are going up. They are the Jeep DJ5. More and more collectors are snapping these up for projects. They can still be found at a decent price but usually need a lot of work.

Figure 3 An Old Jeep DJ5

I own a Jeep Cherokee and I love it. It's comfortable and runs like a champ. It has a few bumps and bruises but has over 230,000 miles and is still clicking along nicely. Cherokees are nice because they usually have enough room for all your mail as well as parcels. They are four-wheel drive and are good year around haulers. They are easy to find in right hand drive versions, and can be had on the cheap.

Jeep Wranglers are nice as well but are a little more expensive. The two door versions don't have the cargo room of a Cherokee but still work nicely. You can get four door versions of the Wrangler in right hand drive. Like the Cherokee they are four-wheel drive which makes winter driving a little easier.

Subaru makes right hand drive vehicles as well. The Outback and Forester are used in the mail service and come in right hand drive models. Small and fuel efficient they are a popular choice for many carriers.

Outbacks and Foresters are all-wheel drive and get around in the snow and ice quite nicely. Sufficient cargo space and comfortable interiors make them a good choice.

Another option is the Saturn. Yes, *that* Saturn. Believe it or not these GM produced cars came in a right-hand drive model. These cars were made from 1990-2010. While the right hand drive models were produced from the late 90's to the early 2000's. They were advertized as a "Post Office on wheels." I have little experience with these cars so cannot say whether they are good or bad. But if you find a good running car within your budget than I see no reason not to grab it up.

The New Saturn Postal Wagon

How to Buy One

Purchasing a right hand drive vehicle is just like purchasing any other car. You want to give it a good going over, ask lots of questions and take it for a test drive. Make sure everything works and does what it's supposed to do. Anything that doesn't is a good reason to negotiate a lower price. Be careful though, you don't want a project. Time and money dictate that they be cheap, easy fixes. Do some research before you head out to look at it if you have time. Find out blue book values and what the most common issues may be for that particular vehicle.

Rust is an issue, especially on the east coast. Get down and look underneath the car at the floorboards. Look for leaks and smoke coming out of the tailpipe. Strange rattling noises coming from the engine are never a good sign. Jeep Cherokees sometimes have an issue when the front suspension gets worn. It performs what is called "the death wobble." You will be driving along at forty or fifty miles per hour and hit a bump in the road and the vehicle will start shaking so violently you think you have blown out both front tires and the wheels are about to bust loose. This issue can be fixed but is something you should be aware of. If the front suspension looks or feels worn, use it as a reason to get the price reduced.

Take your time, use common sense and if you know anyone who knows a lot about cars take them with you. You need a good vehicle to do your job and you don't want to waste your hard earned cash on a piece of junk.

The one thing you must keep in mind is if you don't have a vehicle that can do the job you can't work. They won't loan you an LLV or anyone else's vehicle. You are responsible for your own vehicle: if it doesn't run neither do you.

Chapter Six

90 Days in the Hole: Probation as a Rural Carrier

Like most new jobs you must complete a probation period. The Postal Service is no different, however there is a twist. Instead of 90 calendar days you must actually work 90 days - or one year, whichever comes first - before your probation is completed. That's 90 days worked. Depending on how much work gets sent your way it might take six months or more before you complete your probationary period.

This is an interesting time for many reasons. The one thing you must keep in mind is that during your probationary period you can be fired for any reason - or no reason at all - and there is nothing you can do about it. Even if you joined the union they cannot represent you during this period. You are on your own. The best thing you can do is keep your head down, do your work, ask questions, show up when scheduled and don't make too many mistakes.

It's a tough time. You will have days where you absolutely hate the job and days where you thinks it's not so bad. Power through it. With the Post Office it's the same thing day in and day out. Nothing changes. Those 90 days are important in getting yourself trained, building your reputation with your co-workers and with the boss. You will undoubtedly make the decision during this time if this is a job you want to make a career. A lot will be going on. It can get to you. Don't let it.

When I was first hired, my Postmaster sat me down and told me that it was a very tough job the first few months and practically begged me to be patient and let the job come to me. The first few weeks will be overwhelming and you will wonder how in the hell anyone can do this job at all. You will see regulars who have been working 20 years get a route done in half the time it takes you. It's frustrating. Bare with it.

Your First Week

On your first day a couple of different things may happen. You may spend the day riding along with one of the carriers learning a route and how to do the job. Listen and ask questions. Watch closely what they are doing. See how they organize their vehicle, how they handle the mail. How they service the boxes. All these things will help you do the job faster and more efficiently with fewer mistakes. No question is stupid. If you're not sure then ask. You're better off not trying to figure things out for yourself. It only slows you down.

The next day you may be given half a route. You will help case the route, pull it down and load all the mail and parcels for that half in your vehicle and be sent on your way. The next day you may do the second half...or the half you didn't do the day before. On the third day you will do it all. You will most likely not finish and someone will come out and help you get it done. This will happen a lot your first few months, especially if you get bounced from one route to another and never get a real chance to learn a route thoroughly.

Casing

Casing is the most frustrating part of the job. It is the most likely reason a new hire will give up and quit. When you are a substitute carrier you will bounce from case to case and it will seem like it takes forever before you even have a basic familiarity with the case. Sometimes you will start getting it only to be moved on and not return for months causing you to forget everything you learned. It's a real pain in the neck.

Figure 4 A typical Mail Case

A case is set up in the order you will deliver the mail on the route. It goes counter clockwise around the case until you get to the bottom and the last slot which is the last box on that route. In these slots you will put flats (magazines and catalogs), raw mail (unsorted), and DPS (sorted mail). You will also put markers in the appropriate slot to mark an address where a parcel will be delivered.

Raw mail is unsorted flats and mail. It can vary in amount each day and by office. Our office gets a lot of it and, depending on how familiar you are with the case, can be a real pain to get sorted. Raw mail is mail that is being forwarded, held or, for some other reason, was kicked out of the system and must be sorted by hand.

DPS mail is the easiest to sort. It comes in trays and is in order starting at the top of your case and working to the bottom. You will find some mail that shouldn't be in there and that will be taken to the throw back case. DPS will make up the bulk of the mail you sort.

Casing is the part of the job that will give you the most headaches. It takes time and practice. It takes patience and perseverance. Endure the dark times and the light will shine through - I promise.

What to expect long term

As a substitute mail carrier for the Postal Service there are a few thing that you will have to deal with. They are a part of life working for the Post Office and must become a part of your personal life as well. The late night and early morning phone calls for instance. You will learn to make plans but know they may not happen the way you had hoped.

The first thing to remember is you are a temporary employee. You may work as a sub for years before becoming a regular. I have heard of subs working as long as 12 years before finally becoming a career employee. That might be an extreme example but the point is it might take a while. As a temporary employee you will get little in the way of benefits. No vacation time or personal days off. There are times you will work full time and not get any benefits. It's a huge downside to the job.

Expect your phone to ring the night before or the morning of a day you thought you had off. It will happen a lot. Once in a while you might be able to beg off but don't make it a habit. Tell them no too many times and you will be let go, especially during the first year. Just say yes and go on in. I've had them call me at ten in the morning to come in to help carry parcels for the regulars.

You are not guaranteed hours. You may work a lot or not at all. You really can't depend on your paycheck being a certain amount like you can with a regular job. Often, you have no idea what your schedule will be from one day to the next. It's frustrating but that's the nature of the job.

The one thing they will allow you to do is contact area Post Offices and see if you can work with them on days you are not working for your home office. Many offices are under staffed and this is a good way to get more hours.

Some last thoughts

In many of these paragraphs I have given you worst case scenarios based on what I have seen and personally experienced. Your experience may be different. Being an RCA is not for everyone. But don't make your decision about whether you want to stick it out and make it a career based on the first few weeks or even months. The Post Office is like fine wine you must taste it after its aged a while to decide if you like it or not.

Working for the Post Office can be a very stressful job. You must complete your rounds no matter what and in the time they tell you it must be done. Speed is the name of the game. Your routes are all evaluated to take a certain amount of time and that is the time you must get it done in. That creates a lot of stress, especially for newbies. You must learn to deal with the stress and not let it overwhelm you. Give it time. I know I've said that dozens of times already but it is the one central truism about this job. Be patient.

So is it all bad? No, absolutely not. It's a decent wage with a chance for advancement. Think of the RCA position as a foot in the door position. Once you make regular carrier you will make more money and finally have benefits and a regular schedule you can depend on. It might take a while but good things come to those who wait.

I hope this book has helped you on your quest to get hired or just find out if you want to mess with it at all. Either way, you now have a basic idea of what the job entails and what to expect now and in the future. So thanks for reading and good luck on your journey!